Walking Through Fire

Maggie Helwig

Winnipeg: Turnstone Press, 1981

Published by Turnstone Press, St. John's College, University of Manitoba, Winnipeg, Manitoba R3T 2M5. Turnstone Press gratefully acknowledges a grant from the Canada Council which has aided in the publication of this book.

Cover design by Brian Phillips

Canadian Cataloguing in Publication Data

Helwig, Maggie, 1961-
Walking through fire

A poem.
ISBN 0-88801-061-3

I. Title.
PS8565.E48W3 C811'.54 C81-091311-9
PR9199.3.H44W3

ISBN 0-88801-061-3

to my great-grandmother, Rosina Abbott

Summis desiderantes affectibus, 9 December, 1484

The witches must be burnt.

As by God's word they burn in Hell forever
so then by ours
shall they burn on the earth.
For we who wear the fisher's ring are named and bound
to tend the lambs in all the world
as here behind our walls
and the outer darkness daily grows more great.
That all may turn to us and to our God
these witches must be burnt.

(Do they then burn for you,
Giovanni Battista Cibò, born of Genoa,
Bishop of Savona?
No
not for me.
Our hands are clean;
we are
the Innocent)

Johanna Weber, "The Witch"– District of Trier

That they would come in darkness I had known
black men with hooded eyes and hands of stone
the servants of the jealous thunder-god
who dwells beyond the world, and all alone.

I saw the trees drip blood the night they came
they drove their horses through it as through rain
and then they knelt before their god to pray
I heard the fire as they spoke his name.

Conference in the Church

As I am sure that you appreciate
our labours for the faith
and that you as a judge can understand
how arduous our duties may be as
Inquisitors of Upper Germany,
my colleague and myself shall demonstrate
how in the civil courts you may proceed
against these witches.

That is to say, we shall lay out for you
our several methods,
questions on the matter,
and those things else
we feel you should consider
that you may function here
as we at Mainz.
It seems that in this way
we may exterminate the witches
with the greatest ease.

May we proceed
upon this understanding?

Walter Kuyper – The Judge

The houses of the town are square and safe,
a fence against the dangerous forest
and the far wild mountains – here
I keep the law in rooms with even walls.
I am a churchgoer
I worship God, and flee in fear
the vivid Devil.

And now these witches dance with him at midnight
and lie with him in bloody lust till dawn.
I have learned that I must watch for them
they could be anywhere
their masks are clever.

Red as hot blood and black as night they foul us
I wait, am careful, keep my daughter in the house at night.
And I in Jesus' name will cleanse this town

the testimony starts tomorrow.

Johanna's Legacy

You who were quickened when the moon was full
my blood and body, subtle as the grass,
you who were passed through fire by the Goddess' hand
you shall be more than I have ever been.

We have perhaps a few days more
until they come – then I
will burn. But you they do not know.
Elizabeth, you must not die.

And now I give into your life from mine
the power of the stars of blood and ice
the power of the rue that heals and kills
that you, child, may survive.

Diocese of Trier, 5 March, 1485, In the Presence of Me, Roderich Sette, the Notary of Said Diocese, Before Walter Kuyper, Judge of Said Diocese

The witness Martina Kirschke of the diocese of Trier was called, sworn and questioned concerning the accused Johanna Weber, called in the village the Witch, and did state that said accused had come to her husband Andreas as he lay in fever, and giving him certain simples and calling upon the names of demons had caused the fever to cease; and further, that she had seen said accused with a child and believed her to be the mother of this child, having conceived her as she lay with the Devil in the form of an Incubus.

Martina's testimony having been advertised, Johannes Brandt came forward and did testify that said Johanna Weber had passed through his field and three days later his cow did die, and that he had seen her in a tempest and could hear her laugh, as if she were pleased this hail should fall.

The Judge of the parish, deciding that Johanna Weber lay under strong suspicion of witchcraft, did issue an order for her arrest, that she might be put to the question.

Arrest of a Witch

Cover your eyes as you come
and do not speak
        (they burn themselves into the night
         with staves of fire)
Wear a cross and bear the Blessed Wax
        (the doors the walls
         seven times seven
         circles broken)
Search all places for her instruments and tokens
let her not go from your sight
        (crushed on the floor
         the bitterroot for snakebite
         alkanet for bleeding. . .
         bleeding from the mouth
         two teeth
         knocked out)
And bind her to plank to take her from the house
that she may not again stand on the ground

        (Elizabeth
         run)

In the Presence of Roderich Sette, Notary of Trier

Johanna Weber, having been taken in arrest, was led before the Judge and instructed to repeat the abjuration of heresy read by him to her, and to profess her faith in the Holy Catholic and Apostolic Faith as taught by the Holy Roman Church. When she did remain silent and would not respond to the diligent examinations of the lawyers, she was sentenced to be kept in strong durance, fettered and chained, until such time as she would confess her error.

Martina Kirschke was once more called and sworn for questioning concerning the child whom she had seen in association with the said Johanna. She did state, however, that she had seen said child conveyed from the area by a man on a black horse, whom she did believe to be a demon.

In accordance with the instructions of the Judge, the officers of the court did bring before him all those crippled or afflicted with leprosy or diseases of similar nature, that they might be questioned. Those who could not, under examination, give an account in proper order of the origin of their affliction were judged to bear the demonstration of traffic with the Devil, and were accordingly sentenced to the flames.

Martina Kirschke

The child is still within me – women of the village
tell me it should move.
I am afraid.
Andreas says the witch would know.
He is deceived that she did seem to cure him once.

But I fear now I feel the punishment of God –
I lied about the girl.

I cannot quite say why –
I know that it was wrong
but she was young, and I could see no harm.
Probably she will not live long anyway.

And I have done God's work.
I gave the witch to them
and know that He is pleased.
My secret after all is not so great –

but I am frightened by this waiting silence.

Elizabeth

voices, voices
smell of fire, smell of death
village women
black as ashes

            and I am young
            I am too young for this

      the herbs my hands
      they burn me
      violet leaves
      that I may not go mad

and through the bones of night
the fire
through the fields
black bones and always voices
bleeding eyes

                        I do not know
                        I do not know

         Mother, the world is burning

Andreas Kirschke

I have never seen such things as this.
They took the witch
and now they swear the town is full of devils.
Their eyes are hot as drunken men's
they walk too quickly.

So strong they search for demons that it seems
they long to find them
and a more wicked thing than that I do not know.

Perhaps they have forgotten
in the Pestilence
only the witch could turn aside the sickness.
Martina, I think, trusted those priests too far

she never learned
that sometimes there are questions.

But I am not a fool that I will touch their foolishness.
I will let them be till they are sober.

Johanna in Prison

I do not fear so much now for myself
for I have always known that I would die this way.
But not my daughter, not Elizabeth –
she must not fall to them.

Even here sometimes I feel her moving
and there are two fires on her now.
I have seen her growing bright as fever
and I know the Goddess will demand her soon.
She must live
and she must find the seeing
that she needs beside the sight.
But the dark men now know her
and the night
the night, Elizabeth, is dangerous.

She must not grow to her own curse
and must not fall.
She is the bearer of the Lady's fire
but can she pass through fire with it whole?

Question VI – How the Trial is to be Proceeded with and Continued

Now it is beginning
now they start to understand.
After the first arrest the people came,
came freely to me for the Bible and the law.
Now five more women stand accused –
one, shown machines of torture, has confessed already.
Another hanged herself
we were not vigilant enough.
The rest have been imprisoned.

Already I can start to see the village clear
simple as letting blood for sickness.
God may be pleased to look upon this town

the woman will be burnt, I think, on Sunday.

Kirschke House, Saturday

Andreas, for our child's sake
do not do this.

If I could see the burning of a witch
it might remove the curse
from off my womb.
Tomorrow they will lead the first one to the stake
for all the world to see,
and you would keep me here?

She is old, and we
have never spoken to her.
Her husband raises chickens, cheats me at the market.

It is important
that I should be there.

You do not understand, Andreas.

Churchbells – Elizabeth

and every hour death and death and death
they praise their god with noises in the sky
and grind the shining earth beneath their feet

something there is that I must do
pick goldenseal at dawn
steal food from houses of the dead
survive

and they walk heavy on the sacred ground and break the circles
and cannot see the stars as stars
and every day
they murder holy things

he laid hands on the seamstress in the street
and she turned black
and broke into a million pieces
and I ran

and all the bells will ring forever
voices ask me who I am

I am a child

In the Presence of Roderich Sette, Notary of Trier

Elena Rabethge, having been put to the question for two days, did confess that she was a witch, and, when questioned concerning her associates in this craft, did name Hilda Eydt, Renate Jagow and Claudia Hahn. All this she confessed freely, and was not under the stress of torture when she spoke.

The three women aforementioned were taken to be kept in custody. The said Renate having been accused also by one Patrizius Hess, she was considered to be gravely suspect. Upon her refusal to proclaim herself penitent of heresy, she was sentenced to the flames.

The said Patrizius Hess, after his deposition to the court, was himself accused by one Katarina Schmidt, that he had caused the milk of her cows to turn so that she could not make it to yield butter. He was accordingly taken in arrest that he might be put to the question.

It was brought before the court that Johanna Weber, under frequent examination and the first degree of the question, had not responded in a satisfactory manner, but did repeatedly deny what the court knew to be the truth. The Judge did accordingly order that she be exposed in moderate degree to the engines of torture.

Claudia Hahn – Prison of Trier

My God, my God
what do you want from me?
My sin is great, I know,
for Thou art just
and if Thy hand must touch me so –

they say I am a witch
and if their words are Yours I must believe.
It must be true
or there is nothing left to trust.

The names they ask of me,
the others
yes it must be so.
I do not know –

there must be someone I may name.
Surely You would not guide me wrong in this
and let me pay with this at least –

forgive me, God, what for Thy will I speak.

Elizabeth – The Choosing

between the fence and forest, voice and fire
they have me caught

to see them die, to see them
walk the streets and rot
and moon and voices will not let me run

never I wanted this
never I asked
how can you bind me by promises
I never have made?

night is dangerous, light
is worse
their eyes are after me

but something is here that I must find

calling me closer, closer

I will take up the promise
but was I only saved to die?

The Judge – The Service of the Lord

If I must be the knife of God, so let me be.
And if this be deep-buried, I cut deep.

So well they hid, so many
and before the trials I never knew.
Only the torture shows the devils out
that we may strike.
I see my duty well
and pull this thing up by its dripping roots

and if this goes so far
then so go I.
I shall not see my daughter live
among such stain.

Andreas

The barn is warm with the bodies of horses,
familiar with their smell.
And outside there is terror.

I never thought
that I would hear Martina beg to see a woman die.
I never thought these things would come to us.
It has all turned so strange.

All the empty houses.
Renate now is dead, Claudia Hahn,
I do not even know how many more.
Our child is sick within Martina's womb
and the doctor has delivered women only twice.
Always the witch –
but now she is not here.

I am more tired than I could ever say.
I had not thought that night could fall so fast.

Prison of Trier – Johanna

To give them no excuse.
They will break me
take my name and turn me mad,
make me nothing, kill me only then
but I will not let them believe
that they are right.
From me they will not have what they must hear.

I know their ways
and this at least will not be easy for them.
I must remember –
not what is right
not what is true –
that they will kill me even if I speak
and there is nothing more that they can do.

Nightwatch

Andreas says all pregnant women dream.
My mother fears the devil, and she prays for me.

And every night I see the witch's child
in barley fields and frost
with seven different leaves around her head
and red moons in her hand
and every night she speaks to me
in words I cannot understand.

I wake to pains within my womb
and yesterday
my hands clutched plants that were not there.

And it is not the devil
nor my silent, heavy belly
that sends these dreams to me.

Erce, Erce. . .

The Judge

The filth within this town!
Oh Lord my God, do cleanse me of these things that I must hear
My courtroom is a black confessional
but there is no forgiveness.

They tell me of the Devil's lust,
of dancing by the moon, of spirits in the earth.
These women, they are found out by their blood
that they cannot be clean.

Before they foul me I turn myself away
unto my God who bears no stain of earth
and to my daughter
my white child who bears only her innocence

and only need forgive the sin that brought her life.

In the Presence of Roderich Sette, Notary of Trier

Johanna Weber, having given no good account of herself under the lighter forms of torture, was sentenced to continuance thereof to a greater degree. The Judge did order that she first be shown the machines for use in this torture, that terror of these might induce her freely to confess.

Maria Emmerich did come forward and volunteer that she was herself a witch; that she did possess three demons, one in the shape of a cat, with the name of Holt, and two in the shape of weasels, with the names of Beelzebub and Heart-of-Cheese; that she did often fly through the air to meet with Satan; and that she had caused three people to die in the past year through witchcraft. She did further state that Katarina Schmidt was a witch also, and had bewitched the cows of Martina Kirschke.

The said Maria was sentenced to the flames, and Martina Kirschke was called to confirm the charges on Katarina. However, in the course of the questioning she did begin to travail and was conveyed from the court.

Johannes Brandt did state that he had had conversation with one Hans Eichardt, and that the said Hans had made known to him that a witch had, by some manner, deprived him of his virile member, and that he believed this to be the work of one Julia Wintzen. The Judge did issue an order that she be brought to the court, that she might be examined.

Delivery – The Kirschke Child

Blood, blood

it is not time

and fire in me
hands of heavy ice and pain

not right, not right

black blood and what –
my child –
wrong, wrong

nothing that can be done

no cry
and I
am twisted
broken
and there is no help

the witch would know

no
no
Andreas
no

The Naming

the stake and seven stars
and I am here before this hill of bone and grey

powder of flesh
hot on my feet like thorn

raise hands and pour it on my head
and curse myself with this blessing
from the dead

I bow before the fierce red flower at the heart
and voices, voices

I among the ashes am Elizabeth
she who must learn the name to call the world

In the Presence of Roderich Sette, Notary of Trier

The physician Dieter Weishaupt did declare that, as he did attend the birth of the child of Martina Kirschke, said child being born dead, her husband Andreas did state that the witch could save it. Anna Jagow, sister of Martina, also present at the time, did confirm this.

The said Andreas was called to the question on this matter, and did affirm that he had so spoken, and had been in earnest when he spoke so. He was sentenced to the flames forthwith.

Eulogy

My Christ, what I have seen – Andreas, oh Andreas
they tied the weight around his neck
and held him on his knees before the church
he would not speak
they took him to the courtyard
and I heard it from the house –

and now the world is empty of his hands
the cold air slaps on my bare skin
and, God, I lay with him,
carried his child –
Andreas
Lord, where is he now?

Then has my body pressed a witch's flesh?
No, no!
And my dead child
was no witch seed –

but, oh my Lord, could you be wrong?

Why is the earth not steady
underneath my feet?

The Executioner's Prayer

My Lord, today we burned five women
and a girl of twelve
who had bewitched her uncle so that he did die.
Lord, I have served you well,
have turned my eyes to you
and scorned this world of dust.
I know full well
the task that I am given.
In thy works I must be strong.
But grant your servant, Lord, this prayer –

please do not let them scream so long.

Johanna – After the Question

The world is very simple now.
Four walls
and pain
and black-robed men whose flesh is full of ash.
I vomit their holy water
and I lie
in my own blood –
until I speak their truth
they will not even let me die.

If I could know these men,
if I could understand what their god means
he that they say will have no part of earth
that they say cannot bear the very quickening. . .
the god they speak of is too strange.

and all I know is that they fear
the snakes, the bloodroot and the moon
and they have taken all these things from me
and left me here alone.

In the Presence of Dieter Weishaupt, Physician of Trier

Katarina Schmidt, when exposed to the very gentlest question, being suspended hardly clear of the ground by her thumbs, after she was set quite free, did declare openly that she was indeed a witch and had injured many cows. She did also state that Anna Jagow and Julia Wintzen were her companions in this craft. She, and the said Julia, were sentenced forthwith. The Judge did rule, however, that Anna Jagow was suspect only lightly, and she was accordingly taken to be put to the question.

Hans Eichardt did depose that, on the death of Julia Wintzen he was freed from his malady, but that now his wife's milk did turn and he did think this to be the work of one of her associates in sorcery.

Ignaz Bibelheimer and Jakob Strauss did separately state that they knew Antonie Sette to be a witch, and that her husband Roderich knew this also but was concealing her with intent. The said Antonie and the said Roderich were accordingly sentenced to the flames.

The Judge – Prison Visitation

I hate this place.
And I have never wished to see the torture.
I have no taste for their strong poison
and I do not need further views of Hell.

It is too dark and wet
and smells too strong
and prisoners creep pale like maggots under rocks.
This is what waits beneath my feet in court
and this may be what waits beneath the final day.

We have made these things on earth
for God who made them at the last.
If this is then a truth
then this must be

but never, when I come from here,
do I feel clean.

The Summoning

it is here
it is here
and I Elizabeth am here
and I do not know why

                                I came at night into the town
                                and worms were in their flesh

        hunger teeth at marrow
        and mad songs of voices
I knew that it was here that I must be tonight

all wooden walls and straw
and I

                    one day I picked the mallow root
                    and understood the speech of birds
                    and now

words, my own words
I do not understand

Witness – Martina Kirschke

And every step I take
the earth collapses underneath my feet
and every day more women disappear
and I no longer know who I must fear –

to hear a voice that calls me to the barn
is no more mad than all of this.

There in the corner was the girl
still as a snake
and I bird-captive in her eyes.

The neighbours would have come if I had called
but for some space
the spinning world was still

and then she turned away and dropped
her head into her hands;
she ran.

Devil's seed
we are both guilty.
Yet

Elizabeth, you must not die.

Judge, Courtroom of Trier, Night

All is vanity
all
is vanity.
Satan, thy traps are clever;
these forms
these outward painted lies.
And all are only clay.

We executed seven more this morning.
One they had said was the most beautiful girl
in Upper Germany.
With her head shaved, she looked much changed.

My belly is dust
my heart black bile.
Oh, my daughter, let me see
my innocence in you.

Sentence Delivered to Johanna Weber, Prisoner in Trier

We, the Judge and assessors, having attended to and considered the details of the process enacted by us against you Johanna Weber of the district of Trier, and having diligently examined the whole matter, find that you are equivocal in your admissions; as when you say that you did cure Andreas Kirschke without resort to a compact with the Devil and yet without the help of God. Wherefore, that the truth may be known from your own mouth, and that henceforth you may not offend the ears of the Judge, we declare, judge and sentence that on this present day at the seventh hour of the evening you be placed under the furthest degree of the question and torture. This sentence was given according to due process by the officials of the court of the district of Trier.

The Question

Not even a body
but a thousand deaths
within a bag of skin.

The twisted throat, the burning breath
that lies and gives no air
blood bubbling in the chest
iron red-hot on feet that cannot move
the legs are gone
bones and veins a paste in the wedge
and splintered through the flesh.

Hot blood salt in the mouth
and vomit
wrenching from the belly
tearing of joint and muscle, limbs that will not answer.
The bones no longer hold together
only the chains
keep all this in one piece.

I scream for them to kill me
and they turn their backs.

Martina Kirschke – Resolution

No more testimony.
They will have no words from me.
No more.

I am guilty too, and I no longer know
what things are real.
It is all falling like dead leaves
if they knew true
they would have burned me long before
and not –

if God is with them, God has lied
and that cannot be so

but where He may be now I do not know.

This is some new sort of questioning.
I never answered questions well
only when I knew what I should say

this is too hard.
Is there no quiet place
where I can stand and say that I am safe?

And will the girl come to me again?

Elizabeth – The Fugitive

something is falling on me
with terrible wings

hide in the forest, hide in the hills
hide from the voices and the awful hands
hide from the woman in the village
asking something and I cannot stand
the pain of it

they are burning, burning
and they smell of hate and fear
voices are closer
I can almost
hear their words –

I do not want it!

the worm was not in her
I saw

she was not burning like the others

sounds and silence both are hunting me
I know not who will win but know
that I will not go free

In the Presence of Dieter Weishaupt, Physician of Trier

Anna Jagow, having been put to the second degree of the question, and being asked to name her associates in sorcery, did give the names of Maria Emmerich and Claudia Hahn, but was rebuked that these had already perished. When shown machines for the continuance of the question, she did confess that she knew Margarethe Kuyper, daughter of the Judge of the district, to be a witch.

After she gave this testimony, Jakob Strauss and Johannes Brandt did come forward to confirm the charge. It was concluded that said Margarethe must be considered both suspect and defamed, and she was accordingly taken that she might be questioned.

On being led into the room where machines of torture were displayed, she did freely confess herself to be a witch, and continued firm in her confession through questioning by several reputable men. When brought again to the courtroom, she did at first hesitate, and then did freely repeat what she had said. She was sentenced accordingly.

Johanna

I heard you from my cell
and then I knew.
The rot is in you,
filth is crawling
from your amber silence –
you would kill your seed!

You eat your blood
and spew it
on the cycles of the world.
The circles turning backwards,
all the rings are broken now
and we are lost on paths
that only can go straight.

And now you lead her past my cell
and well I know to where.
And broken by your hand I say to you
you are the only blasphemy there is

and you will pay.

Judgement

They led you in
and you fell on your knees and spoke –
and then I saw that we are born
the venom of the snake
and life is sin

My child

The flames around your feet were golden
and in the smoke
He purified your heart.
And now you rest

my child, my child
bones white as the garments of Christ.

That broken thing they called the witch
is almost gone.
The town will soon be clean.
I have fulfilled my mission.

Soon the flames of Heaven shall come
and shall redeem us all.

In the Presence of Dieter Weishaupt, Acting Judge of Trier

Hermann Eischkind, assessor of Trier, did state that, on passing the cell of Johanna Weber as he led a prisoner, he did hear her utter the words "You will pay for this." It did seem clear to him that this was in reference to her powers of witchcraft and so did constitute a confession of guilt. The said Johanna was accordingly sentenced to the flames.

Following his arrival to conduct an examination of the proceedings of the enquiry, the Archbishop Johaan von Schoneburg did conclude that Walter Kuyper, Judge of the diocese, was guilty of leniency to a degree harmful to the safety of the Holy Roman Church. When brought into court to respond to these charges, the said Walter would make no good answer, and did at one question openly scorn the said Archbishop. Accordingly, after excommunication from the protection of the Church, he was sentenced to be tortured, strangled, and then burned.

It was agreed that after these executions the enquiry would cease.

Trier – Final Execution

can truth then be no more than burning flesh?
oh mother
ashes
ashes
crackling skin
and all these things are finally what is left

                and bells
                the voices
                moonblack, starblack
        herbs that wither
        in my hands

                Erce
                mother of earth
                they broke you in these flames

and I am young
and cannot speak my name

        my mother, I have failed
        and do not know
        what I was asked to do

Martina

The trials are over –
I am still alive.

I am the only woman in the village.

All gone, all gone
the bones are buried in the woods
to have survived
I must have been the greatest witch of all.

And it is time.
The flames are in me now.
The death is growing in my heart

another time
and I
the greatest witch of all
will join my ashes with the rest

forever

and forever. . .

. . . and all the bells will ring forever
shining earth beneath their feet forever. . .

never
never. . .

it is over. . .

No!

Baptism

No! No!
I am Elizabeth,
I live, and in me You do move
as seed and fire, Lady of the Night!

For You are earth and breath and blood
and are forever.
And in the burning You are flame,
consumed You are the ash
and cannot die!

Lady of flower, Lady of crimson claw,
by this your moon
by this my blood
I now am Yours –

I now
am You.

Circle

And she is in the field
with night behind her.
And I go forward to her.

Witch's seed
I am Martina.
I share witch blood.

I shall never speak to you nor touch you.
After this night we shall not meet again.
You hand me herbs
and I do not know what they mean.

But this I know –
I turn and I return,
and, witch, we are the same flesh,
you and I –

I shall not burn.

Selected books from Turnstone Press

Marsh Burning by David Arnason
Mother's Gone Fishing by Norma Dillon
Soviet Poems by Ralph Gustafson
This Body That I Live In by Anne Le Dressay
The Raw Edges by Dorothy Livesay
Lacuna by Laura McLauchlan
The Cranberry Tree by Enid Delgatty Rutland
No Country for White Men by Gordon Turner
In the Gutting Shed by W.D. Valgardson
Mister Never by Miriam Waddington